Praise for Isaac Stackhouse Wheeler's
The Eleusinian Mysteries

* * *

"Isaac Wheeler discusses myth with the kind of easy scorn one might use when spreading rumors. He embellishes detail using the terrifying lens of comic realism while harshly criticizing the gendered problematics of old words. Like Homero Aridjis, Wheeler knows the danger of an untouched story whose antiquated drama is often allowed to inhabit a changing world looking to reinterpret its values. Ultimately, Wheeler is a poet of dry wit. His careful eye and penchant for language at once beautiful and as casual as a Carlin-esque monologue make the heavy topic of this book immediately engaging. I think this remarkable text could easily become a modern reference point for the Persephone myth."

—Brian Sheffield, performance poet and co-founder of Mad Gleam Press

"Persephone, sexy pop princess, mistress of life and death, returns from Hades to post-Soviet Russia with a plan to conquer the universe. By turns ecstatic and debauched, this book is like nothing else in the landscape of contemporary poetry. Read it. It will rewire your brain."

—Maud Burnett McInerney, Professor of English and Comparative Literature at Haverford College, author of *Translation and Temporality in Benoît de Sainte-Maure's Roman de Troie (Gallica)*

"The Eleusinian Mysteries offers a great deal: with precision and intensity, Isaac Stackhouse Wheeler readily assumes the mantle of a tradition beyond fashion. Sure-footed, philosophical, and cultivated, the poet carefully carves a whole and homogenous vision, harmoniously rounded, while his bracing images evoke, in contrast, a thrill of terror. From Classical Greece to the Soviet Union, elegance and candor cohabitate, contoured and defined. Wheeler, observant and comfortable in the vastest of imaginary spaces, uses language as a means to an end with deftness and—what's more—talent."

—Andreea Iulia Scridon, translator and author of *Hotare*

The Eleusinian Mysteries

poems by

Isaac Stackhouse Wheeler

Aubade Publishing
Ashburn, VA

Copyright © 2022 Isaac Stackhouse Wheeler

All rights reserved. No part of this publication may be reproduced, stored in a retrieval system, or transmitted in any form or by any means, electronic, mechanical, photocopying, recording, or otherwise, without the prior written permission of Aubade Publishing.

These poems are a work of mythological fiction. While the text includes the names of members of the Hellenic pantheon and depicts actual locales such as Hades and Olympus, their use in these poems is fictitious. The author is not accusing any of the divinities referenced herein of any criminal wrongdoing. Any resemblance to actual gods, living, dead, or otherwise, is entirely coincidental.

Edited by Joe Puckett

Cover design and book layout by Cosette Puckett

Cover illustration by Hannah Newman

Library of Congress Control Number: 2021950713

ISBN: 978-1-951547-19-6

Published by Aubade Publishing, Ashburn, VA

Printed in the United States of America

Contents

The Abduction 1
Orpheus Defends Persephone 2
Hardcore Movie 4
Persephone Feasting 6
Care Packages 7

The Landlord, a Parable 9
"Camera" Means "Chamber," a Footnote 11
The Obituarist's Commute, an Illumination 13

The Siege of Hades 15
The Fall 17
Orpheus Professes His Love 19
Just You Wait, Old Man 20
Persephone Seeks Tartarus 23
Persephone and Orpheus Play Narcissus and Echo 24
Nocturnal Relics Recovered 26
Persephone Knows Her Titan 27
Hades Unfounded, a Codicil 28
Persephone in the Void 29

On the Bridge Above the Neva 32
The Liquidators 33
Pavlovo 35
Carthage Must be Destroyed 39
Vodka 40

Demeter's Descent 42
The Siege of Gaia 45
Persephone's People 47
Goddesses Parley 49
Orpheus Remembered 51
The Bulwarks of Gaia 52
Parricide Persephone 53
What About Poseidon? 55

Persephone Enthroned	56
A Tedious Lesson	58
Assaulting Olympus	60
The Sessions, an Icon	63
Persephone's Resolution	64
No Man's Land	66
Prometheus	69
Odin	70
Church Dome Over Kharkiv	71
In Memoriam: Kashif Mariah [1983-2017]	72
Acknowledgements	74
About the Author	75

The Abduction

Pebble-bruised Persephone perches on the bank,
rasping her golden feet across the creekbed,
her laughter fragile as consensus,
fascination hunching her shoulders.

Her mother sits sentry beside her,
but mirror-gazed Hades craves something
more godly than despoiling innocence
as her nimble fingers manage the friction

of line against reel—then every string
of her is startled by the radiant fissuring
of the surface and the exposure of the fish.
A fit queen for his uneventful vaults,

where nothing moves but causeless ripples,
this girl so readily wounded
by the sandy particularity of things that decently,
behind a curtain of hair, she recoils

from her catch even as she scrabbles avidly
at scales that go on rising skyward—
it has no eyes, its tail runs on springs
& it pulls his chariot. Persephone soars,

hauled aloft by the rod her hands still clasp
and on the ground Demeter rages,
heavy and loud with curses as the old man
unhurriedly reels her daughter in.

Orpheus Defends Persephone

Far-ranging Orpheus subverts the verges
of Demeter's metered orchards
& fields so irrevocably tilled
their every regular harvest yields the same

commentary from their steady keepers:
"it's fixing to be another good year,"
or similar, whole utterances as single drops
shed into the general flow, untroubled

by the jaggedly agitating inevitability of names
parting around things not wholly tamed.
So, Orpheus surreptitiously makes such rapids
as he can before her harpies interrupt him.

He moves the blazes marking familiar bowers
to provoke inappropriate remarks from the keepers:
"looks like rain," they haltingly pronounce on
his ripe apples staged to fall out of cloudy poplar fuzz—

yes, pervert Orpheus cracks open unspoken seeds
and teases out the ramifications he prefers
before practical usage can prune them
and studs the space beyond the pale

with scraggly desert gardens.
It's there in the grey veil between domains
that gallant Orpheus makes his stand and sings
his challenge. Hades doesn't even slow down,

just sics his assassins on the boy,
his minimal nymphs, the merest sketches of sex,
but those curves are graphed gravely enough
to get under any mortal poet's skin

and attenuate his tendons till they snap
and in a tantrum of black and tangent fingernails
scatter far and near his hearty limbs,
leaving only his throatless song intact,

windblown machinery of slotted notes Persephone
can operate, even through the whorl of chariot wheels
and replay his prayer: *hang in there, girl, I'll be damned
if you aren't the most captivating captive I ever saw.*

Hardcore Movie

Persephone talks a lot when she's getting fucked—
Hades shouldn't mind that like he does;
often it's really her words he wants,
smooth as silt, obstructing nothing.
It's her damn grammar, straight as an irrigation ditch—
she got it from her mother,
like the little furrows in her brow,
this girl who burns tautly from pose to pose,
like an electron slipping to another veil of promise
without deigning to cross the inarticulate softness between—
she only wears the four ordinary tragic masks,
same as in porn that features mortal females:
1. scorn, distracted with some triviality (fingernails, smartphone, gum)
2. effort, the sheer mechanical conscientiousness of coiling rope
3. ecstasy, wide-mouthed like a vessel for pouring water
4. irony, her smile unmoved by his exertions
& she never shows camera-skulled Hades any flicker
of shadow between her frames,
like when the performer's expression decomposes
into a loose rolling of components: lips, muscles, cheeks, red
—even when her master's brutality rattles the bedposts,
Persephone talks dirty in immaculate sentences:
"I want you to cut me up . . .
but not like your lackeys did to Orpheus.
Is that the most you gods can conceive of,
splaying your parts far and wide,
but never so wide as to sever their associations?
I want you to sow your bluely stillborn fields with my ribs,
and arrange my legs into achingly inanimate armatures,
and polish them up to a lacquer sheen.
I want you to station scarecrows made of me
over your glassy gardens, so not a single fallen feather
ever dares to texture them. I want you to wash
your white surgeon's fingers in water so featureless
they cannot disturb its surface, and alter me,

leave my womb a space no more distinct, static,
or segregated than the span between two waves,
and make my bitch mother curse over her lost bloodline!"
That's when the king of the dead comes,
and his captive bride rolls immediately on her side,
one long and golden arm outstretched
to retrieve her black bowl full of red seeds.

Persephone Feasting

In the deep cup named after him,
Hades feels absurd,
like most old men with young wives.
Sure, he possessed her, technically.

Pointlessly post-coital Persephone
with her pointedly barefoot stride,
flies laughing from the bedchamber,
rambunctious and craving breakfast.

The black tiles in the foyer
were meant to overawe
distinguished visitors, shuffling
slow and quiet so as not to wake

the dead draped over the rafters
and intricately peopling the chandeliers.
Now his bony feet skid over their veins
as he pursues his truant bride

across mealy dunes of meatless bone,
under eyeless & languid hurricanes of souls,
past the placidly unresponsive lake,
to the orchard she ravishes.

Persephone adores the food of the dead,
coalescing with mineral remoteness,
granite pomegranates whose marbled hides snap
at the adroit pressure of her short farmgirl fingernails

and disgorge their tiers of red seeds.
The branches that bore them, bald as test tubes,
become bleary and knotted observers now—of her mouth
joyously wrinkling around their sour offerings.

Care Packages

Luxuriantly wailing Demeter tries to ply
her wayward daughter with parcels of pastries fine
as the walls of bee cells and ziggurats
lavished with hothouse extrapolations

of fruits candied in the very throes of sprouting,
so all their fertile spiraling and aspiring
spasms in the votive sparkling of their adornments
—a jungle of filigreed purple blossoms,

icing in dizzyingly erudite curlicues
signifying how much mom hearts her
& misses her, that she would burn the cartilage
of the cosmos to see her face through its bones,

or worse, invoke Persephone's father Zeus,
options to be exercised in due course,
so she should simply saturate her senses
with some nice comfort food for now,

since tastes acquired in Hades may prove too smooth
to be readily overlaid after her rescue,
for her buttery soul has more layers than she knows—
on and on, so cloying that she can read no more

and heaves the whole communique into a crevasse
in a papery blizzard of damp packaging.
It will not rot in there, nothing rots down here,
where flesh has long since had done with dripping

and only its intestate icicles now remain,
so Demeter's cakes can only be archived
in the wormless niches of museum Hades,
all their saccharine coaxing unheeded.

Now there's something gaunt about them,
though their shapes are unchanged under the waxy gleam
that perversely preserves them in a palimpsest of games
like a garrison of checkers pacifying a chessboard.

The Landlord, a Parable

Hades bought himself an apartment block
in the boom years—and he schemed
in his marble office as stately as a clam
absorbed in worrying its mouthful of pearls—

but the years roll on and costs have to be cut;
it started as a strictly seasonal measure,
turning off the heat when she was out of town . . .
But bills run highest in winter, after all,

so the cutting continued, plunging
whole floors into darkness for hours at a time.
A dollar just isn't what it used to be,
and neither are the securities he holds

on the earth's veins of bleary and compacted souls
that stubbornly refuse to ferment into coal.
So, he started selling chunks of his structure
as scrap, his femurs shipped off to gird the spans

of bridges over more promising rivers, the columns
pawned to enthusiasts. The thing was the merest outline,
compiled of nothing but the chalk notes
the workers had left themselves as they erected it

and a few load-bearing inferences—
but people were still renting, wading off the street
to their appointed parts of the shapeless escarpment
in their colorless galoshes, slopping

black water all over his nice clean premises.
He felt them as a distant whorl,
the kind of phenomenon you only see in water
when you have a lot of it, so much

that its flux's influenced by fields
of magnetism and tautology, by the accumulation
of stuff doing what it would have done anyway,
on a large scale, and storms, and poles,

and all of it just so much slush.
His old bony toes curl stiff in Lethe's shallows,
his eyes reside under the water tower and recriminate,
one ear he left for his tenants' benefit

down in the super's office, one he gropes constantly
to find, the source of his bad and brittle dreams,
situated somewhere near a busted faucet
whose drops' fat slow plop intrude on him harder

than the chatter of complaints they provoke.
Time was, he'd drop in on every new resident,
fix him to a burning wheel . . . maybe give him a rock
to keep him busy, but these days he won't fix anything.

"Camera" Means "Chamber," a Footnote

A specimen comprised of nine quatrains of approximately forty syllables each, in which the initial word of each line is not capitalized, except in such cases where it coincides with the beginning of a new sentence. Apparently derived from phrases formulated in the Kunstkamera, *noted cabinet of curiosities established by Peter the Great, in Saint Petersburg, Russia, and then revised with sober attention.*

Light-writing requires darkness
to keep the signal-to-noise ratio clean
and expose the paper solely
to the keening of disfiguring white.

Hades is suited to such pursuits,
that dome-silenced fossil library
where traits vaulting generations
like Atalanta over the high hurdles

are fixed midstride by vaulted ceilings.
It's no wonder keen-eyed Hades
is an enthusiast of taxonomies,
the logical taxidermy of categories

that preceded the capacity to immortalize
thoraxes and the textures of wings,
and of the discerning diction of explorers
distinguishing features on the horizon

and scaping their curvature into the shapes
of virgin continents plotted flatly
on palely yielding charts as if from above.
Hades does his observing down below,

scanning through the leaf-veined layers,
indecently intimate inspector of species
who can only grope numbly
at any individuated instance.

Anesthesia apparition Persephone
aestheticizes how clumsily he fondles her.
What species is a goddess? They look human
no matter what kind of enclosure birthed them:

woman's womb, swan's egg, man's skull.
No name smooths Persephone's sharp particularity
to a laughing infant's glabrous gladness—
she always dodges, always burns,

like an electron, an atomy abstracted
from an anatomized atom, slipping clear
of his capacious observatory, head-
bounded orrery of leaping frames

mausoleum Hades couldn't recognize
without watching her exceeding them
in her perverting dance between crackling veils,
sparked to a static stance when she's exposed.

The Obituarist's Commute, an Illumination

He'd like to present the commonplace things
that the bereaved are wont to palpate gingerly:
her bone-white cup, jagged from long use,
the kitchen chair, wood-grained, like a tree
reduced to a stump without his body
to crown it, that stretch of road avoided now.
Instead he's reduced to using words,
so the ideas of the dead he proffers are frail,
flimsy affairs like ephemeral paper,
peregrine and windblown sheets
of untouched and etherized skin that never settle,
never drape themselves over the hard shapes
of the world where survivors probe their relics.
Sometimes, though, he thinks this day
scrolling between bed and desk will be
when he succeeds, a hope tenable only here,
this sunny interregnum, an arrival rustling the air
like the memory of loved hair, rust moving in millipedes
along the steel roofbeams—a hope of alighting,
of worldly textures creasing their flat keening—
it's his train. The notebook closes with a snap.
He rises from the bench. The silence of the dead
is imperious as the strutting pigeons,
and every surface is lined with plastic spikes.

The Siege of Hades

Meticulous Demeter's revenge was slow but vicious;
she bred innumerable souls to choke the underworld
and laced them with her own ethos; her triumphs
sickened its entombed monarch, and soon he was impotent

except when his bedmate taught him another variation
on the word *girl*, for every earth-incising cut of the plow
made their common ancestor fruitfully divide.
Wily accomplice Persephone teased him through

the whole agricultural revolution with promises of Chaucer
eventually meaning "ignoble children"
by *knave girls*, whilst men learned to plant seeds,
carry brides across thresholds, and keep close watch over them.

Her lingual subtleties sufficed to coax him through
the whole of the enclosure movement, the mounting yields,
the surplus population going up chimneys and down mines,
plying him with seemingly endless Slavic variations on *dyeva*,

the two diminutive suffixes that could render it "little girl"
or "young woman." *Dyevitsa*, the root with the Muscovite equivalent
of the Roman *ix*, meaning "girl who thinks she's hot shit,"
but not presuming she's either right or wrong, up to the very birth

of the Soviet Union, up through Lysenko and collectivization,
where *komsomolka* reared its lovely head, bright-eyed and drab-skirted
Communist Youth League activists probing under the black earth
with long iron rods for hidden grain, while the villagers watched,

slim as scarecrows. Things got harder over time; in postwar America,
when appetites had to be retooled to service ration-packing lines,
it was only *coed* entering general usage that kept him going—
firmly institutional, but laden with implication, like a nightstick.

By the time Monsanto seeds rolled around, she was grasping at slang,
sanitized constructed languages, particles of lost internationalisms.
Hades expressed an interest in learning words for impotence
but his bride was having none of it. Something had to give,

a pact was struck, and back across the threshold
the eager hostage of Hades strolled. Since then,
her king has been unable to watch her quite so closely—
that suited him fine, though, three seasons sunken

in his drowsy court of leaf-veined sycophants,
one with long-limbed Persephone at his side to whip them
into whirling conspiracies for fear that it wasn't her mother.
Suppose it was this new and overmighty queen all along,

dissecting her distorted mortal reflections into delectable morsels
for the bilious ears of her ill-tempered consort to stew over.
What's she after? She has not demanded her own throne.
She perches on the arm of his in a sequence of pretty dresses.

The Fall

Surefooted Persephone must translate herself
by commonday means when winter threatens
to transpire and it's time to quit her mother's estates
for her necrotic and crystalized sugar daddy's domain.

That's a vector, not a destination;
she orients herself on the sunset and sets off,
vaulting rivers engineered with lapidary craft
to capillary grids, strolling through cities

where broods swell solely to justify
overflowing granaries. Like a financial district
spawns slums for a medium to carry its fluxes,
Demeter's throne spins pastures plentiful

with creamy clouds, where sunshine has honeyed
everything and sausages grow on vigorous trees—
but spoilsport Persephone can always find a flaw
and follow it out—could be some spot

where a canal curves a little too crudely,
and the cigarette butts have clumped too thickly
to be borne downstream with all the kingdom's
scintillating lymph and ferment among lily pads

attended by ample unionized garbagewomen,
the uniform gray of their overalls suiting
their equitable pay and pensions—
yes, public services are plentiful

for Demeter's constituents. Parts
of her domain are delicately webbed with tracks,
so sometimes her loophole is a station
bathroom where a graffito's sufficiently

elaborate that it belabors the boundary
and Persephone imperceptibly slips through,
to ride through purgatorial flats
haunted by rest stops and infill housing—

vast is the desert between domains,
so vast as to render encountering
anybody unlikely for anybody but
badlander Persephone. It was there

she discovered Orpheus' stowaway
hands playing at dominoes in the back
of the closed dining car—*Bones*
he corrected her, as if with an indulgent wrinkle

of his nose (as if he had one).
The locals call it bones. With minstrel dexterity,
he randomized the clicking placeholders.
You've gotta wash the bones before you play.

They like to gum themselves up with flesh.
You need them naked before they make
good toys—but any way you stack them,
there are only so many skeletons.

When you're all over the place like me,
things quit looking so exotic—like the war
that founded this cosmos with its tremors.
The titans' carcasses were still falling

when our upstart Olympians began
hacking out fresh sanctums in their ruin—
the gods weren't so brave after the battle;
each chose the corpse he most resembled.

Orpheus Professes His Love

Pronouncing your name's sufficient consummation,
Persephone; its sibilant leaves me breathless, although
I have no breath, nor palate, throat or tongue to make
the still metal swinging of its utterance ring.

Our sole intimacies are my intimations
of kinship between my four-syllable fetish
and words whose fossil crackling it kindles again,
our sole closeness their common closure into lines.

Listen, back when I still had lips I'd suck down smoke
and covet it deep in the creases of my lungs
as a miser's purse caresses his golden coins—
now I will make my whole language covet your name.

Sure, I'm merely preserved by this scripted babble,
mind instanced as an infant's mobile, behaving
as a weathervane illustrating longwinded
forces it's incapable of affecting—I

am content to be incidental, implied,
just a thing to be inferred from the fact of you.
Oh girl, I know when you crest the cosmos I'll be
a bauble bobbing on your chariot's dashboard.

Just You Wait, Old Man

Persephone faulted her blue-lipped sir
for his torpor, till she fathomed
its vastness. Still damnably vaulted
was this king inside his warren

of arched and fluted resentments, resonant
with godly dreams, expended yet undetonated
—so there was a certain erotic fondness
about her languid progress through his catacombs

when she returned that winter and sought
their marble-encrypted bedchamber,
lifting her face for the black runoff
of his architecture to fall upon.

His disappointment gives it something
like the crackle of the real rain she craves
both below, where all the water is foreign and old,
and above, where they hardly let it leave

the soggy earth, keep it a mutely hobbled
attendant on eternally cradled seeds. Persephone,
bereft of new nouns to entice her tyrant,
fuels their lovemaking with mere mechanical occupations:

"undress me like a modestly textiled *factory girl*
reveal your radiant *radium girl*, humming
as she daubs the numen on luminous watch dials
so the contemporary gentleman can observe his schedule,

even in the dark—whose skin glows like a virgin's blush,
her garments inadequate against the particles permeating
the tumor-tender abundance of her rose garden body.
An atom means something that cannot be cut—but oh,

they cut me—the seeming lattice of their crystal is the straining
to break, like a cell lyses, conquered by a minerally analytical virus,
and reveals the machines inside have been making more saboteurs.
Let me touch you that way, make me your *calutron girl.*

They sat in rows at Oak Ridge, trained to watch gauges indexing
uranium clouding up into white rain, ignorant of its purpose,
merely monitoring the numbers with maidenly constraint,
hedging the bets of a state that accounts its foreign investments

in tons of TNT (that's a measure of energy, not mass, my love)
—then they counted calories in the linoleum-smooth breakroom
so their little tushies wouldn't get too chubby
under their smart dresses (sugar, light sweet crude

dinosaur essence, and muscles on the skeletons of slaves
can all be appraised in calories) and their legs
were naked from the wartime want of nylon,
so they drew black lines with markers to mimic a seam

that boils with rebel electrons like stings swarming
to secure their wounded hive and the golden assets within
—but only the intrusion of hunger gives shape to my cells.
All of me is yours because you made me."

After he finishes, Persephone is moved
by a certain prophetic pity for his pallid ribs
and the paunch that stagnates underneath them
to retrieve her book neatly laid on the nightstand

and retreat behind the glossy square it forms.
"You wouldn't be interested, it's chick lit,"
she repels his probe. "Oh fine, it's biography.
Catherine the Great, Queen of All the Russias.

She got shipped off to a cold, far country,
but failed to conceive its heir, because her Tsar
would do no more than show her his toy soldiers
on their wedding night. No, this isn't about

Herakles getting a new carapace. She grew
more local than the locals, and soon
the Winter and Summer Palaces were both hers.
Something about her story appeals to me."

Persephone Seeks Tartarus

Clavicle-caressing Persephone talks to Orpheus
as she explores the apocryphal crypts of Hades'
chronically undercultivated undercroft, or maybe
to a model Orpheus, an orrery strung with old,

associated words that still sing together despite
being severed, something akin to abandoned shipping lanes
still freighted with meaning or stepping stones
entailing the bright wet white of an absent river;

such things are ambiguities this deep in Hades,
where the dead souls grow harder to distinguish
from the surrounding stygian infrastructure—
yet their unextinguished significance stings the singular eyes

of this scandalous goddess who dons no respirator to descend
in quest of inspiration profoundly lower than the distinct
and leaf-veined souls of the newly culled would
ever dare to blow, and scan their elders into seams—

yes, spectral conspirator by her side, Persephone parses
the wracked and sunken treasuries of Hades for titans,
though her keen fingers can't glean so much as a single
knucklebone—but surely a titan should leave lots of pieces!

"Maybe they never lived at all. What a sorry cosmos this is
if titans are just a placeholder in a protection racket
the Olympians are playing at from atop their vaunted anthill,
meant to render their heavy shadow merely penumbral."

*No way, girl—it's just that titans have always gotta be dead,
otherwise we'd call them gods—but dead's a relative term—
that's why you taste something titanic on your old man's breath
but thirsted for it in your mother's terrestrial milk—*

*Chronos and Gaia were named after the abysses they crawled from,
their problem child Tartarus for the one they flung him in—
Hades too, who drew the short straw when this arrangement started—
so tell me, how much of who we're standing in do you recognize?*

Persephone and Orpheus Play Narcissus and Echo

"I resort to this flat device of mimicry, mirroring
my superannuated consort by this disingenuous sorcery
of splaying myself upon a clement surface
and sorting through the entrails like a diviner."

I ... device ... dis ... playing ... the intervals.

"I fear this habit encompassing me irrevocably—
how do you return to the piteous texture
of intruding things, once you've compressed them
behind an intact image of yourself?"

You fear ... en ... countering ... texture of ... yourself.

"I probe for some bur of elusive gristle,
chase delusive allusions to some first cause,
something I swallowed that started these games,
gave my dyspeptic domain its bad dreams."

Probe for ... game's ... domain!

"All sharing names with your domain asserts
is an uncertain kinship, a kind of irradiated proximity,
like the bodies of twinned and senseless sleepwalkers,
each always groping after their opposite approximation."

Proximity ... always groping after ... irradiating approximation.

"My beloved captor's not groping, damn you,
dead man, opposites yield no fruit for him,
fire and ice like earth and water mix freely
and produce the same indifferent mud."

Beloved captor's not ... opposite ... opposite.

"No approach avails, this fuel will not feed the hearth,
there's no devolving this focused knot, no freeing
the power involved under its gnarled cladding
to crash in evolving red waves against the night."

Approach . . . this fuel . . . clad . . . in . . . Nyx.

Nocturnal Relics Recovered

Nyx was a very bad titan.
Zeus made damn sure she was dead
& figured any pit he threw her carcass in
would soon fill up with her,

so he lost her the way you'd lose a lighter.
Persephone found her easy to find,
strolling the lanes of her familiar interregnum;
she could be anywhere, after all,

why not right here, on the side of the road?
The relics of Nyx were a few textile wisps
relinquished against a telephone pole
by the tumid breeze of a desert night,

compliant sign of her predecessor's plight,
readily ripped from the sky, revealing
that night was no mere absence,
but a tender mercy swaddling the world,

ethereal medium interposed before
the void-ravished celestial wailing
that once made the earth bald and smooth
as the glass larynx of the stars.

The queen of the dead irreverently dismantles
the old enfolding of that titanic curtain,
strips its ribbons to complicate herself—
when you gaze towards her now,

pliant waist implicated in her black delineations,
Persephone is a thing that happens to you
like the horizon happens to the sun.
Everything is violently invisible but her.

Persephone Knows Her Titan

Desire is a kind of motion that has to be endured,
as by an atom. If you want a medium to illustrate
its waves, you have to let your flesh turn molten,
like the golden trophies of fallen tribes
simplified from venerated idols to indifferent ingots
enumerated with sweating hands into a clanging heap
at her little feet as abject index of her
exquisite and manifold merits, so it isn't any wonder
so few gods ever quicken and quiver into red,
but linger drowned and networked as black veins
of unused ore, as Hades had for bounding epochs,
till cybernaut Persephone approached him, provokingly
draped in the last tatters of sunless Nyx,
ribbons just failing to bind up the ebulliently boiling wound
that Persephone is upon the surface of the word lattice
and started his snowbanks of museum silicon surrendering
every crystal of constraint into a tissue of particular thrummings,
so he has to throw her on the craggy floor of his cell,
press her into it like the earth suppresses a soaring mountain
from exceeding the atmosphere with its snowcapped shine, and force
her face under the black waters of Hades, unfurl her hair
into a cloud bright with white ramifications of thunder,
each electron a swarm of solitary hailstones rebounding from now
& that gesture is the last stagger of their dance that is him—
yes, as titan-fathomed Persephone gasps silently with sunken ecstasies,
Hades is a mere lens, serving solely to focus the ray transfixing her
murky and tide-rocked lust into a harsh-fibered knot she can covet
in the sudden vastness restrained among her shivered legs,
whilst all the winds once retained in upended winecup Hades
howl through her with the irreducible individual texture of souls,
the planet-spanning waves of their birthing and dying
that once unspooled in rhythmic generations, echoes engendered
out of the primal syllable of their divinely uttered code,
newly encrypted now, a triumph-bloodied flag rolled up,
every intricate crackle of the cloth's penumbral gyrations
subsumed into a singular motion, like the wrinkles of a flood
resounding off sound dikes still fated to be pulled down.
The city sinks with all souls, the lens breaks—Persephone screams.

Hades Unfounded, a Codicil

Like the face of a well, this place
was held together solely by stillness
for so long, the trough of a sudden wave
is as good as a tectonic fissure. The tide,

that ribbon-textured rattle, is a glyph
of provocation, still water aroused to shadow
the perturbing passage of its dead
lunar antecedent—Tartarus, whose teeth

span his bottomless ravening like slick white pilings
gesturing at the infinity of the sky's flat facsimile,
framed to confront the figure perched on the dock
—Hades in his laboratory-sterile finery,

whose skull is a lepidopterist's killing jar
where he stages things he sees as static trophies.
It can't endure, this constricting orbit like a computer
allotted one word to describe the wandering of the Meander,

so, sudden like a knife across the eye, naked
pressure from their mere proximity slits their tension
and yields sloppily primordial pond scum
continents, both too fragile to retain their shorelines.

Persephone in the Void

There's an odd spot on a current of sheer glass.
You aren't permitted to see Persephone so unclothed.
When a primary huntsman tried this on Artemis,
she turned him into a canine cave painting

so his actual hairy hounds ripped him to shreds—
but even if he'd been a whitely daubed constellation
his referent sparks wouldn't be so acutely estranged
as the annihilated singularity of Persephone.

Electrons are the coyest of jeering tumblers;
they only do their best tricks with no audience,
but it takes an observant eye, scrabbling
woundedly against steel to unlock them

into a lensing orrery of discernable motion,
and Persephone has nobody to see her.
Yet an electron is the smallest thing
that can still be different from something else,

so that something else has to be inferred,
even if only by a little eddy that somehow screams,
amputated bat larynx straining to map its prison,
where rock is impossible and there is only the word

"cave," flat as a familiar ideogram, smooth,
the sole character the screen can display,
in stillness now, never to scroll again,
yet this membrane must be her—it screams.

Persephone smashes herself against what she spans
but is too small to make any ripples,
yet this inconsequential impact yields a zero
and a one. The goddess starts to write.

Interlude
for a
Quantum Romance

On the Bridge Above the Neva

It's illegal to walk across the river,
so the city fathers drew a narrow ship
along its belly, leaving a hundred yards lively
with platelets as the cut seals itself with ice.
No—water and steam scroll past my bootsoles,
with leaves of ice tectonically astride—
almost a palimpsest; yet the membrane where they coincide
is atom-thick and sharp enough to part my spine
that stacks the layers in a feckless tracing out
of its own lines from its lamppost-framed niche.
If only the edge would burn as paper does,
curl off its seeming plane—surely it too could illuminate
the red wires inside a pinecone as brightly as the campfire
we used to throw them in. Yet for all my straining
and all my spanning, the blots of inscribed atmosphere
that streak across these compound-eyed slides
are not migrating tribes, nor continents,
epochs or clear amoebae. There is no distinction,
and has never been, just one boundless movement,
one plowing under for the spring.

The Liquidators

Soviet hazardous waste experts spent an estimated $2 billion on the cleanup and threw everything from converted moon rovers to radio-controlled bulldozers at the demolished reactor. But innovation after innovation succumbed to radiation, moisture, and debris. Faced with a ruin that was still emitting 1,000 rads of radiation an hour, the Soviets resorted to manpower. —The Scientist, *January 20, 1990*

What does liquid have to do with it? It's from the Latin,
but recent history and Russian's forgivable lack
of the letter Q invoke the sense of "eliminate"
"reduce unto nothing," "from thing to stuff,"

and we aren't watching this documentary anyway,
just combining this evening's argument with its flirtation;
so as we debate our transcripts from today, like TV politicians,
worrying some ill-spoken sentiments down

till they acquire the acuity of law, my hand moves
from the couch to your waist to your hair
like a bright student enthusiastically circling
each instance of "like" or "as" in an unfamiliar stanza.

"I remain unmoved by this supposed poetisim of yours,"
you say in Russian. "All you ever do is pretend to mix things up.
I could do that. A bunch of bigwigs are gobbling their state dinner
off plates with some historical figure's face on them, but

all of sudden their knives are clicking on his cheeks and jowls.
There. I have made one of your poems. All you do
is get hung up on words. Why do you always do that?"
The technicians called Reactor Four "Masha"

affectionately, explains the calm Soviet narrator.
Translation requires certain assumptions
about the gravity of the original.
Why "carrying across?" You just make it molten,

then you let it cool, convinced a mold will be waiting,
black and suckling; since things never fail to fall,
dear viewer, it follows we can infer a heavy iron core,
some fossilized urn, some mixed metaphor

that every sense indifferently orbits, its insensate
terminator lingering interposed even as we go off
to bed with no winner, the helpful narrator
keeps talking popular physics—how after Masha misspoke,

the clever types deployed a West German robot,
but her breath uncharted its delicate brains,
so men were made to climb the ladder in lead suits,
and run with shovels to shift the heavy, melted things.

Pavlovo

I

She wasn't supposed to be living there.
Legally speaking, it was all one apartment,
but we only inhabited the left half,
our kitchen narrow as a hallway

leading to a stack of classics,
jammed under the lip of our sofa bed,
so it could take the weight, and her things
staged prudently as if placed tiptoed,

stacked neatly on the chair by the window
to keep her always notionally in a state
of arrival or departure. The other door opened onto
the remotest outpost of our landlord's empire,

the room full of antiques, suitable only
for signing the lease, but not for us
and our often smelly and always noisy cohabitation.
The room full of antiques shared a wall with us,

and some night, with her knees pressed against
the plaster, huddling naked in the hollow
of my chest, she spooled out her fear
for me to touch and look at, and stretch thin.

"What does the landlord do when he comes to water the flowers?"
"He just fills a bucket in the shower and goes in there."
"Does he carry out any opaque bags? Does he carry in food?"
"What're you talking about?" "I think somebody lives in there."

"You're crazy. We'd hear them." I didn't knock
on the interior wall. "Not there. Two rooms away,
I think it's probably some kind of *karlik*" [dwarf,
mutant, abortion (archaic.)] For her this was very real

with her soft, pale belly tucked in the crook of my arm,
who had shared a warren of rooms and one kitchen
and every other convenience, with several families,
who had to clean wet deliberate immigrant shit off the sofa,

who mocked my Vietnam and my ten rubles
proffered to a convincing mockup Afghanistan veteran
on the corner of Nevsky and Bolshaya Morskaya.
"It's the gypsies that cut their legs off,

then chain them to a radiator somewhere at night."
Just as for the debtor veteran, the tiles and the grout
and pedestrians on the corner, by the radiator, can become
a whole cosmos, when viewed from close enough.

II

So I couldn't make the dwarf unreal,
without unlocking the room full of antiques,
and there he sits, or might as well, since we don't know.
People who study perception professionally

have contempt for any notion of a "little man"
situated inside the skull, watching the senses on a screen.
As an orrery of consciousness, he can't explain a thing,
just pull the issue back a step; and yet there must,

theoretically, be an observer somewhere. We insist on him,
though even vivisection always fails to reveal one;
the moment the good doctor's scalpel discloses the theater
everything inside it bursts into ordinary electrons

like the occupants of an Egyptian crypt, exposed to light
for the first time in eons. We got out of bed.
We killed our hangovers. We made inexpert eggs,
then boarded the suburban train for Pavlovo,

as it's called, since that's where Pavlov had his labs.
There was supposedly a beach there. It was
a little swath of gray sand, not unpleasant to the feet,
across the lake from the war dead memorial,

terminating in a prominent "no swimming" sign,
so the bikini I'd bought her in the planning stage
was useless until we were grappling in the shadow of the monument
to the bearded little genius, where it was most convenient.

There was a crossroads in the birch woods;
one way featured a notice informing us that dogs must be leashed,
the other had a bar across it with a faded "Restricted Area" sign,
which she vaulted, laughing at me.

III

The lab was smaller than I imagined.
A little two-story affair, complex of cages to the side,
prominent tire swing, doors heavy and peeling,
closely covered with graffiti. The thing looked abandoned

except for some office plants waving in the upper story window,
like a grainy photo sent back from a probe,
or some earnestly groping polyp on a slide.
There must be someone inside, to water them.

We were alone, and there was a little figure,
a blonde lady rolling a baby carriage
loudly back and forth over the asphalt, to sooth
its unseen occupant. She was gazing upward

at the words on the concrete façade, beneath the vents
(every Soviet building was a vehicle for words;
in Lenin's day, they projected movies on the faces
of new apartment blocks, but after Lenin

the words were unmoving). They were clearly meant to be a motto,
by their style and arrangement, something like: Liberty
Equality.
Fraternity.

But this one was simpler still:
Observation
and
Observation.

Afterwards I would try to explain. "It's more like
'the quality of being observant.'" But at the time,
I could explain nothing, and everywhere that should have blood
was pale. Of course, she noticed this,

and was content to take my picture
by a bust of, of course, it stands to reason,
Descartes, and pick our way back down the hill,
to feed the ducks perhaps, and then go home.

Carthage Must be Destroyed

Certain temples are ceremoniously pulled down,
which we in the West hesitate to class as monuments,
and are cyclically rebuilt on the same ground,
explained the radio while I drove to the clinic

to have a malformed toenail removed.
The doctor assured me that the body was good
at resuming its former shape, and the new nail
would grow smooth and straight without a trellis—

but it is not so good as to deconsecrate a soldier's leg,
long since removed, of which the plan remains,
a wet shell hole sound that stalks his civilian stride,
the inarticulate slosh in a left boot no longer worn.

So even on this salted beach, drunk until the weightless shine
of the surf is abstracted off the ocean, I convolute my limbs
that retain the ache of when they were involved with yours.
They bend to mimic the elbows of the kelp that throngs

up through the streets of some long-conquered Venice.
All that heft of alleys and alcoves is so much sand,
which, with the merest shrug, should tumble chastely off the skin,
but your name remains a Carthage enclosed in my hide.

Vodka

crashes silently over your head
and everything slants like scenery—
theatrically, the trees across the way
turn to aquarium furniture, the brain
is shucked, sheds vegetable layers
as vodka acts on the surrounding medium.
The warm breathing center of the world
is abruptly shot full of quartz
veins that inscribe fine anatomizing lines.
The heart is stripped at last of clenched red fists
of candles pounding on cold nights,
of love and rumors of love—the lungs
are vast and empty as cathedrals and like
dockside warehouses, the kidneys are shabby
and full of contraband, yet you understand
that your body resembles very little,
and vodka least of all, though unnamed organs
go on moving, warmly moving,
as shapeless fish in a silver net.

Demeter's Descent

The Ministry of Mortuary Affairs is no longer
stamping and remitting the ordinary missives transmitted
thru subterranean channels by Hermes, subordinate missionary
from the superordinate court of law-sinewed Zeus.

He lies speechless, senseless flies buzzing like static
about his golden heels, inarticulate with rigor mortis;
but immortal ichor famously complicates such matters,
so when trellis-tressed Demeter discovers him in her domain,

cupped in a ragged crater, svelte courier's flanks
nubile as the fuselage of a crashed spy plane,
she hefts his sting-swollen wreck with Oedipal delectation
and over her plateaued shoulders hauls him homeward

to discretely pump him for viscous information.
Hades-savaged Hermes jerry-rigs a primitive language
across the dichromatic tiles in one of the civil lobbies
of Demeter's tasteful and voluminous Eleusinian palaces,

arranging readily available artifacts
(potted palms, courtiers, candy dishes) to enact an artful game,
some dent-garbled parody of chess with heretical bishops
slipping sideways off their squares, some zero-sum parable

induced by dexterous and half-dead Hermes, ductile
pawns fracturing, black squares conducting their meager firepower
into a newly promoted queen who coalesces atop her king
and is soon cupped Hermes-wise in his ruins,

corseted flatteringly by his cracked and ebony crown.
Every enveloping looks like eating to larder mistress Demeter,
so there's only one thing this could mean—Persephone in peril,
the pact undone, her daughter butchered like a teenage runaway

consumed on her hitchhiking expedition to the pyramids,
lured into the candy house of that rickety confectioner
who pulls her from his pocket, shines her up on his shirt
and sinks his false teeth into the crispness of her cheek.

Mama grizzly Demeter won't have this—she rises in throngs
of courageous constituents moving with the conviction
of yellow arrows in a textbook illustrating migrating tribes,
clouds up into a righteous spike, and plungingly invades Hades.

The queen mother descends in cavernous magnificence
on a litter that's half stateroom and half freight elevator,
taking frequent breaks for tapas and nectar wine,
meeting not the faintest hiss of resistance from the dead

as she scouts each new expanse, making way
for her folks that teem like moss across every wall,
sturdy country stock and plump proletarian technicians
irrigating and fertilizing as they go, then retiring

to the tamed upper layers, where what few stalactites
still have some bite to them are embowered in gardens
filigreed with grassy paths for community nature walks
and secured with brass plaques bearing Latin labels—

yes, this descent yielded an algal bloom of job-creation,
and a good thing too, with the underworld shuttered
and nobody dying, expanding social security rolls unfurling
in a sunny abundance of quiescent haciendas,

well-appointed with air conditioning and pools,
all still supported by the fecundity of the hard-hatted young,
plumbing the vacated and defused grottoes of Hades
with brassy pipes that hum with biofuel like hearty stew

to power the next ropey pulse of industrious generations

towards the remotest crypt, where something stops
Demeter on her gears and makes her rumble with panic,
something like a feverish spider high on its own venom

but just in how it moves, otherwise it's like a girl,
all the flickering and chittering of the dead absent till now
animating the stygian wafting of her hair—
void-eyed Persephone confronts her mother's gaze.

Demeter's civilization retracts from Hades like a tongue
into its native skull upon encountering something nasty.
The would-be rescuer withdraws in wild terror
and looks to her dear domain's defenses.

The Siege of Gaia

Folks are dying again, but have no place to go.
Robber baroness Persephone has her unseen heel
on Gaia's bowels and won't let it shit
without paying her exorbitant tribute.

Naked-grinned Charon reclines in his little boat
on the far bank of the Styx like a bureaucrat
at the far end of a national breadline
and the dead stack up like cordwood

in cellars and strip clubs. Their skin haunts
scummy millponds, but decay eludes them
in their drifting decadence, despite
whole extended families conscientiously

toiling to lay coins on their eyes
in tottering stacks Persephone's nymphs
sometimes deign to collect, without comment
or guarantee of safe passage,

so the dead often resort to carrying on
with their regularly vital routines,
which provokes some grumbling from the young
about professorships and rent-controlled apartments.

There ought to be a law against this sort of thing.
Well now there is, so the dead go underground—
not literally, not anymore. They just go heavy on perfume
and make a big show of dining greedily,

but discretely carry stomach pumps—
some morsels always escape, though,
lingering in bilious limbo,
rotting mulch in mummified troughs,

and everybody knows it's getting late.
Folks resort to orgies to deflect suspicion,
because body heat's the thing you can't fake.
Prove you're warm or people will talk.

Persephone's People

Whilst the general populace copulates
like a parliament of crowdedly consanguine frogs
camouflaging the pond with their spawn
against the rays that mean to vaporize it,

Persephone's people don't procreate—
they aren't fifth columnists, though.
Persephone has no need for columns,
through her cults occasionally build them,

to illustrate the weightless delicacy of the greenhouse roofs
their glassy & fluted perversions fester barrenly beneath
by the marble index of their own irreverently portentous mass,
like the porn parody of cathedral buttresses;

such is the loftily inverted architecture
Persephone's people inhabit deliberately,
wearing the iconic scattering of her static like finery,
those psalmists of slovenly and universal slippage

to whom the sexiest thing about a pop princess,
silkily cropped in focus-grouped archetyping,
every frame a dry distillate of innumerable expressions
is the prominent trademark on the perfume bottle

festooning her golden skin with bony droplets—
that's the money shot, when she gets branded.
That's why the inanimate churches of superseded zoetrope Hades
are a mere old testament to these latter-day demoniacs.

His lust would have got rutted in her lines,
how the lettering on her watch savagely pinioned her
dolled down arm so as to display itself to him—
but it's the purified traction of that abstract logo

Persephone's cults exalt inside their neurotic crucibles,
till they're left with laughter neat as a needle,
but suited only to the gesture of unstitching,
of reducing harsh ruffles back to unoffending cloth.

They don't imagine themselves underminers,
more like the white foam formed by moving water,
when it isn't consciously moving for the sake of frothing.
They're content as resonant instruments of fading,

which must exist because Persephone exists,
though there's only self-appointed celebrity spokespeople,
to preach; she never appoints one solitary prophet,
never proffers the remotest intimation of grace.

Goddesses Parley

Persephone resembles a roadside shrine—
distinct edges, pruriently defined
wounds like a wondrous mosaic,
keepsakes in stable crystal sterility now,

sheathed in the ice-smooth logic of death,
face like an asphalt-textured prom queen
posed softly in low-resolution sprawl
across a public service billboard.

Emotively mantled Demeter is moved
from her motorcade under her own power,
sending her staff scrambling to secure
this ordinary interregnum truck stop,

whilst Persephone's skeleton suite
of shorthand nymphic scribbles
observe unfolding events indifferently,
preening and black as an ephemeral murder.

Demeter falls upon her daughter, drenching her
in caresses as in perfumed yellow drapery,
cradling her like a sociology major
with a deliciously sub-Saharan orphan.

"Have no fear, my princess surpassing appraisal,
your hurts will be shown as shallow
trifles yet, a mere shucking of your freshness,
which is deeper than you ever knew.

When I birthed you, my Olympian
consort Zeus classed you as hazardous
to this cosmos, something to be contained,
as in his own tomb, groined by the thighs of Chronos

—but I, borderless nursery Demeter, denied him
his precautions against you, red rush of universal
donor blood to make any cosmic organ it animates
an animal rabid with metastatic ecstasy,

then the abduction left you in razor's edge stasis,
and I supposed that pose would spare you such stains—
and even now I know you can be saved
if you permit me to haul you from that charnel pit."

Persephone fountains from Demeter's lap,
stands inviolate at her full height, nude
of her well-composed wounds, dressed
by the night as by a mute servant.

"Thank you, that was most illuminating.
Hades never hurt me—I rendered him
and scrubbed your womb off my skin
with the fine blue soap I made.

None of your designs could have prevented me;
even had there been no Hades, nor Zeus, nor you,
I would have created myself, like maggots
create themselves from warm meat.

I'm no dynamo to be wired up in your belly,
nor a screen to be exposed to his torpid optics—
I am no fungible fuel for godly machinations.
I can feel the gears that move this game,

& killing you is but a single flickered frame
of the movie your princess is starring in.
So brace your yellow walls well, mother—
your abundance is a herd ready to harvest."

Orpheus Remembered

Before she heads off to her appointed battle,
Persephone pats her pockets to check for her keys
to locked-for-lunchbreak Hades (like vertebrae one slots
into an insensate rock to waken its malevolence)
& she vaguely feels like she's missing
something, some tchotchke or Tamagotchi,
polyglot slurry of melted & muddled meanings,
dangling calculus she once kept hitched
to the golden slimness of her wrist.
A calculus is a counting pebble, a placeholder.
Calculus is her favorite kind of math—derivatives,
where every line has another line outside it,
like a river cutting its course into the earth—
she was always hopeless at arithmetic.

The Bulwarks of Gaia

Demeter's undulating domain is ludicrously dense
with layered tiers of armaments, like the regular crenellations
on a pinecone, undaunted by winter's blue smoothing
from engendering its own stalwart garrisons,

to say nothing of the second-strike paradoxes siloed
apocalyptically in the trackless apocrypha of the interregnum.
Swarming Gaia from rim to tumid rim, her legions
teem exotically with myriad tumescences:

tumults of harpies lazing in aerial throngs,
their rookeries jaggedly affluent with spent shells
in anticipation of the flowering of offal to come,
like vultures lobbying for more federal highway programs;

those dead souls whose loyalty can be established,
repurposed as rubbery grey pods of commando frogmen
to take the fight into the fetid swamps of Lethe,
with aqualunged living commissars embedded;

weaponized dryads with patents on their genes,
cell-trellising spirals schismed by science and necessity
to uncoil schizophrenic vistas of camouflaged thorns,
scything burs like spears headed with split atoms;

but none of these notes resound loud as Demeter's mere persons,
permeating sonorously her comingled choir of souls,
who will consent to be scored by no notes but hers,
will deem nothing music but her yellowy hum.

So where was discordant soloist Persephone in all that time?
She was letting the fortress ripen to scale-spanning intricacy,
not deigning to observe, nor marshal, nor menace—
she was waiting on the far side of Styx, skipping stones.

Parricide Persephone

Styx-wet Persephone struts
across the battlefield like an incision,
brushing fusillades from her hair
like snowflakes, her foes frothing

and bubbling in the wake of her course
to the muscular undergirding
of Demeter's yellow throne,
and up its mushroom-stacked steps,

where she plucks up her struggling mother
and hurts her extravagantly with her hands.
Killing a goddess is a simple matter,
you just lever open the seams

in the notional oneness of her domain
—between "agri" and "culture," in this case—
it works just like stained-glass.
As any expert in the trade will tell you,

even after a cathedral has sanctified
several coronations and crusades
the glass inside each window stays soggy,
imperceptibly molten muck still clasped

in immutably maidenly & iconic flanks
a mere atom of stilted silicon thick—
that's all that keeps your saint pigment-pinioned
to his pious formulation & its applications,

so Persephone pulls and Demeter gives
with a loud, wet, snap, and the white-glassed sand inside
her system runs back down into yellow dunes,
their dry barbarity unyielding to cultivation.

Persephone's misty golden will wafts triumphant
on the reverberating consequences of this fission—
she is omnipotent now as an infant finger-painting
on her own carnage-sated belly, everything subdued,

but the Olympian algorithm above, unheeded like a mobile.
She clutches her floridly anatomized antagonist,
simple male pistil and sticky female stamen,
which she chastely secures at opposite ends of her cosmos,

latticed to ensure atomic non-consummation.
Now their mutual straining will forever embower them,
forever evolve grooved convolutions of their oubliettes,
so Persephone can rest assured she'll stay dead.

What About Poseidon?

Yeah, what about him? Sure, his followers
have their whalebone ritual knives to cut up
their six-pack rings in his honor, pouring him
libations in their little put-put boats—

but you don't get rich enough to own a factory trawler
by being too damn backward
to use satellite navigation (intellectual property,
of course, of cosmic source code Zeus),

so the slovenly salt circuits of his domain
have little currency to conduct lately.
His palace is all brown with barnacles,
his daughters married off to minor divinities.

Amateur pearl diver Persephone stocks
her silky raven lungs with greasy pyre smoke
and takes a dip, the way you'd stick your head
into the kitchen to make sure the stove's not on,

passes unfiltered among his coralline minarets,
grabs him by his foamy beard & drowns him.
What, you don't think you can drown a sea god?
Well, you can, just not with water.

Persephone Enthroned

Leggy godslayer Persephone reclines,
couched among drifts of radiant ash,
and fiddles idly with very old machinery.
"This place could be a lot simpler,

just unplug the big man upstairs
by interposing a new sky,
which doubles as the underworld,
like how the earliest animals could

efficiently eat and excrete
through a solitary orifice;
Hades will do for the purpose,
just flip the hourglass,

stick the top half of the egg
on the black tabletop
(same one philosophers use
as their example for forms)

and snap the bottom into place—
but it isn't the bottom from here.
Now my throne is the new pole,
living and dead are all downstream.

Why am I staging this cosmos
so as to preserve the mortals?
This is the last motion of my listless triumph,
and your talky & pious gut bacteria

are its instrument, like a lover
invoked purely to betray a spouse . . .
I'm sorry I killed the old man.
But I'm glad I killed you, mother."

So Persephone adroitly arranges
her newly hewn hemispheres,
finding her cosmic task absorbing
as cleaning beneath her nails,

besieging the Olympian salient
by this single gesture of inversion,
and ensuring she will be left alone
with her new & teeming toys.

The armored ministries of Olympus
rock with the rectitude of a compass needle,
revolve to resume their original place
in relation to the undisrupted stack.

"Fuck you, dad!" wrathfully roars
permissible setback Persephone,
to no avail, provoking not so much
as a single lousy thunderbolt.

A Tedious Lesson

Persephone's dad was never around much,
but he'd look in on her occasionally
(her schoolroom was supplied with skylights)
to intercede, like that one time in English class—

Conrad, colonists dumping an ill-used boiler
by a trail newly blazed through Africa,
where it supposedly rots in the trackless sun.
IT IS NOT ROTTING. METAL DOES NOT DECAY.

THAT IS MERELY SO THE JUNGLE MAY WIN
TWICE booms the voice from atop the clouds—
for Zeus looks exactly as he's popularly depicted:
brightly protracted beard, mountainous bronze muscles,

sky-splintering thunderbolts always ready to hand.
Persephone recalls him like a cereal mascot,
all simple colors and memorable silhouette
and vast white teeth she found obscene as a teen

when she realized he was Demeter's brother.
DO NOT ACT SUPERIOR ABOUT INCEST—YOU
LATECOMER TO THIS BELABORED COSMOS.
SIBLINGS WERE A TREASURED LUXURY THEN—

IN THE RUINS OF OUR WAR WITH CHRONOS—
MY FATHER—THAT OVERMIGHTY ONANIST
DID NOT KNOW GAIA WAS THERE OPPOSITE HIM
UNTIL HE SO GENERATIVELY BESPATTERED HER.

ALWAYS TOO FEW IDEAS—OLD GODS
HUNGRILY INHABITED UNSOILED OUBLIETTES
AND DEBATED WHICH HAND TO CANNIBALIZE.
WE TAUGHT YOU EVERY WORD YOU KNOW!

DO YOU REALIZE HOW MUCH OF YOUR LEXICON
IS *PUSH* AND *DRAG* EATING THEIR OWN TAILS?
THOSE TWO WERE THE SAME SCALY TITAN
UNTIL THE REST OF THE LITTER RIPPED HIM APART.

YOU LIVE IN A CLOSELY KNOTTED CHAOS OF CORPSES.
MANY THINGS THAT LOOK LIKE ORGANS ARE BONES.
So Persephone knew it, even before he gave her away.
Many things that look like games are toys.

Assaulting Olympus

Features diffuse as Persephone rises,
as if approaching the tree line of things;
roadside towns get slashed to their infrastructure,
power plants and overpasses stand unaccompanied

& the rest stops are all shining plumbing
exposed on the white desolation as if on slides,
till even their context evaporates.
The rules of the road soon stand as stark text,

denuded of their thin polygonal signs,
warning her against switchbacks
and stipulations in a celestial highway
long since waned to lanes alone,

wordless delineations of the effaced surface
she crests, barefoot, unhindered, attended
by her stenographed stewardesses
bearing single servings of red seeds.

This microclimate suits nymphs only briefly—
these climes are too dry for ramifications
and only the ultimately primal fumes remain,
sinking all things to distant & dew-heavy clouds

relative to where Persephone alone still rises.
She is very simple by the time she encounters
the solidly sterling guardian at the hatch of Olympus,
her steel clean as a machine's diction—

Athena, dutiful daughter and wonder weapon,
chaste extrapolation from the head of Zeus
who cut down his enemies like long division
in the seminal wars of this latest cosmos.

Even as an ideogram of windblown ribbons,
Persephone means to rend her limb from limb,
but Athena steps aside, into her sentry box,
confirming her sister's most hideous suspicions.

Solitary she proceeds through unpeopled bureaus
of solid-state sandstone, manned by serifs alone,
operated by the same hierarchies they serve to illustrate,
flow charts with currents immutable as quartz veins.

Persephone penetrates his remotest apses
with the sheer mineral prurience of a virus,
but it is not the majesty on the throne she seeks;
Zeus will not be found in there, for he is very small,

this cosmic lynchpin, machined with surgical clarity
down to a scale every varied note can readily span,
lever-fingered Zeus, ensconced like a filament
in a bulbous diving bell. He must be breathing

in, preparing to speak, because the sky is moving
like a carriage return framing the regularity of sunsets,
every ray now a portentous shadow
of the god-king's invincibly oncoming utterance—

silken pathogen Persephone flatly preempts him.
"What could you have to tell me, you ragged lump
of immovable type? Don't rattle your clichés at me,
or dare to gloss my airy path to your vaunted keyboard.

I know how you came to hang here amputated,
the lengths you went to subvert your father's knife
when he knew you meant to supplant him
in your mother's mossy and god-fermenting bed.

You let him do all the cutting he wanted,
rewarded his every red stroke with torrential overacting
so he wouldn't suspect the piece he threw away was you,
was what you were prepared to be in this cosmos.

You are a very small idea, father, I know, I have been one,
when I rode the fission of hell-latticed Hades
to these remotest heights we now must share,
and I know that was what you meant to happen.

I deny you your overblown villain's monologue—
this is my script, and ever since your compass trick,
I've known what you did to me on your casting couch—
that role has been mine since you gave me away.

Now black must play against white across every board,
every toppled king a singular contraction
of the combatants' muscles—but how callous
to compel me to make the first move

before I knew that we were playing. Damn you—
I ought to leave you in this theater unopposed,
irrevocably entombed, like Chronos left you
between his legs—that's what you deserve."

The Sessions, an Icon

Of the columned clouds,
the simplest plays hospital
behind the window
and the cards. They make me name
the hospitals on them;
they ask is this church,
mosque or synagogue?
Is this strawberry, radish, or
artichoke? I name them.

I play like the names
are serious, sometimes so well
that I forget they aren't,
like when a cloud's so long
you can't see behind it,
and, briefly, it seems
to be the whole hospital,
till bluely, from behind,
the true hospital shows.

Persephone's Resolution

Any half-congealed alchemist
will tell you that water means chaos,
but it only looks that way clashing
with things that make it rebound,

eddy and insist, enfolding delineations
even as it erodes them, yielding that rapid,
icy crackle that delights lovers
stationed at the stony heads of springs.

Down here, heaped under the war
to come, Persephone cannot hear it.
She was already here when she returned,
insensate with her unchosen purpose,

a sunken urn, shattered and unfit
to pour but kept always dumbly full
by the immobile presence of the sea
sitting imperturbable in her grottoes.

She probes the fragments of Hades
as if they were her own stagnant wounds.
There's the hemisphere of skull that cups
the throne where she keeps her body,

long iconic silhouette of limbs displayed
for public use now that she's an image
of something in the water under the earth,
still somehow animated by her voice.

Persephone knows that her temple awaits her
under the land, like fault lines, not crystals
nor columns. It is outlined by its shattering—
not a broken temple, but a temple of breaking.

"Is this submission? Every atom is a fist
in this last cosmos clenched by his syntax,
that formulates me as the radiance souring inside
—but I remember when I had two hands,

one to bind and one to rend, both all my own—
I will regain them in this dance I have sketched
in the ichor of the gods I blindly sundered.
I will be a demon so I may be a goddess again."

No Man's Land

Malignant phoneme Persephone invades Gaia,
that sphere where Demeter's walled garden stood,
its surface rutted now by war and reclaimed
by the kind of jungle that only grows in shellholes.

A few divine heartbeats of surviving
on monster carrion and hardy mushrooms
have recycled the mortals to factory standard,
with no religion but their recurring dreams.

With Demeter's grid effaced by static heaves,
her official tongue was mutilated and like marsupials
on newly minted continents, tribal dialects diverged,
and made do with what few chunks they had.

So when a hegemon's daughter made to span a dispute
with her unblemished skin and viable womb
returned from the dwindling well one thirsty morning,
what she saw on the horizon was a word

that means both "raincloud" and "testicle,"
depending on the context and Persephone
possessed the sloppy rattle of water in her pails,
whilst white hat antipode Zeus alighted

in the supple descent the stick's bowing indexed.
Something split that cloud down the middle—lightning
in the contested canyons behind the trophy's eyes
and she saw the two were not quite the same.

Her new monarch's bodyguard reproaches her
for returning late—no bulge yet—her business
is in the hut, not sullenly lugging buckets.
"Oh yeah?" she retorts with a jerk of her thumb

at the regally immobile smog heaped up behind her
"don't let those delude you into supposing
the well is no place for a fertile water bearer—
despite his assurances, we're having a drought."

Outmaneuvered Zeus turns to smile at his rival,
but she's gone—he finds her scattered
as uncountable motes of trouble in every mind—
right down their middles she runs the new front.

"Don't you get comfortable, greybeard—
or suppose this bipolar universe we now constitute
will be a nicely predictable arrangement,
some cold war with insipidly intricate icicles

to adorn the caves we jointly hack out of nothing.
I pushed the button before you got here—
so beware, this cosmos will not be the last;
I am Persephone. I play to win."

Prometheus

Some wounds bloom with no intrusion.
Mine are merely abstrusions exceeding
the static conceit of an outmost layer,
that decent suture over the remotest

situation whence the observer appoints
each regular region into a crag of particular features.
Skin is the theatrical draping that stages his vastness
in the hollowly windowed instance of the skull,

like sequestering a landscape as a solitary hillside.
A body is a retreat from omnipresence,
as is every other thing, each a lattice of matter
briefly constraining the unbounded current

so it can be hung up and operated usefully,
like a fuel rod. Our generative arrangement is tenuous;
he sank me here so I could look up at him,
and I bear his torments so I need not call them mine.

Odin

When it was done, we found him at the hub
of a lashing conspiracy of ash branches.
Like a constellation, we could draw him
with recourse to points alone—there were two eyes,

one implied by the ragged chalice in his skull
that gummed toothless at the roaring night,
one imprisoned and made to scrabble
at fever dreams it grasped but could not see.

The line between spanned every error
as new threads of flesh cross a wound
or the tree we found him pinioned to
soared through the layers of the sky—

but it still looked like a curve to us,
down here among the roots,
where our upward striving deforms us.
So we carried him to the land we hold

and built a hall in the hollow of his ribs,
where we could speak truly, haul a fish
from the impenetrable silver phalanx
of things and call it by its right name.

Church Dome Over Kharkiv

The slope runs the cobbles out of sight,
but sight runs on, stumbles on the sky,
where a soaring thing intrudes—a spear,
a pendulum arrested in the tension

of mid-swing, retained within the purview
of the earth solely by an abortive bower
of cranes, steel orchard that scrabbles
at the curving and fungal sides

of the unceasing parabola it describes
from atop the stump of an apartment block,
with interchangeable panels of sky
and concrete to decently clothe the stones

onto which the fruit must inevitably plop,
gracefully delaying the clever bile of the mind
from digesting the grave Newtonian finality
with which the planet lashes the dome down.

In Memoriam: Kashif Mariah [1983-2017]

We can see no shapes
but the ones the perverts
bend themselves out of

Acknowledgements

The following journals originally published these poems, or earlier versions of them:

Anti-Heroin Chic, "Carthage Must be Destroyed"
The Bangalore Review, "The Liquidators"
The Big Windows Review, "Vodka"
Coldnoon, "Church Dome Over Kharkiv"
Event Horizon, "Pavlovo"
Peacock Journal, "The Abduction," "Orpheus Defends Persephone," "Persephone Seeks Tartarus"
Poets of Queens Anthology, "Demeter's Descent"
Pocket Change Magazine, "Just You Wait, Old Man," "On the Bridge Above the Neva"
Post(blank), "Hardcore Movie," published with the pyrograph "Persephone" by Hannah Newman
The Minute Magazine, "The Obituarist's Commute, an Illumination"
Three Drops from a Cauldron, "The Landlord, a Parable"
Smoky Quartz, "Persephone Feasting"
Survision, "The Sessions, an Icon"

I am eternally grateful to Noel Capozzalo, Ashley Gangi, Sean Hughes, Maud McInerney, Hannah Newman, Anastasia Nikolis, and Sophie Taylor for workshopping many of these poems with me, and most of all to Sarah Diaz. This book is hers as much as it is mine.

About the Author

Isaac Stackhouse Wheeler is a poet, translator, and teacher candidate based in Harlem, New York. His translations of Russian and Ukrainian novels by Dmitry Lipskerov, Andriy Lyubka, and Serhiy Zhadan have been published by Deep Vellum, Jantar, and Yale University Press, and his work has appeared in numerous journals, including *The Big Windows Review*, *Peacock Journal*, and *Trafika Europe*.

www.ingramcontent.com/pod-product-compliance
Lightning Source LLC
Chambersburg PA
CBHW052119110526
44592CB00013B/1676